Crazy by the letters
Mental Problems from A to Z
by Joey Chou

Choo Choo Clan
Publishing

Copyright©2006 by **Joey Chou**
Text and illlustrations copyright©2006 Joey Chou
edited by Mario Chappell

©All rights reserved.
No part of this book may be reproduced in any form
without written permission from the publisher.

Published by **Choo Choo Clan Publishing,**
www.choochooclan.com

Design by Joey Chou
This is a work of fiction. Names, characters, places,
and incidents are the products of the author's
imagination or are used fictitiously.
Any resemblance to actual persons (living or dead), locales,
institutions or events, without satiric intent,
is entirely coincidental.

Library of Congress Cataloging-in Publication Data available

ISBN 10: 0-9788670-0-9
ISBN 13: 978-0-9788670-0-3

Printed in Taiwan

First Edition

For my mom, dad and sister

Enjoy the book!
Joey Chou

This book belongs to

{ _____ }

Adam is **Autistic**

he gets to see lots of amazing things that we don't.

Autistic - A neurological disorder. Patients show little or no interest in other people. It seems like they live in their own world. Their communication is abnormally developed leading to poor social interaction. Even though autism is a genetic condition, the cause is still unknown.

Benjamin has **Bipolar Disorder,**
you never know what mood he is going to be in.

Bipolar Disorder - Also known as manic depression, the disorder is marked by dramatic mood swings. There are usually two different categories of symptoms, Depressive and Manic. Both are almost opposite to each other. This affects patient's thought, judgement, and social behavior.

Chris's Conduct Disorder
has given him an infamous name of bad boy.

Conduct Disorder - Kids who have conduct disorder tend to have aggressive and destructive behaviors toward other people or animals. Serious violations of rules is also a major sign for conduct disorder. Significant symptoms emerge during mid childhood through mid adolescence but may occur as early as preschool age.

The gloomy weather doesn't seem to help **Danny's Depression.**

Depression - When mood gets so low it begins to affect eating, sleeping, social behavior and thinking. This is not the same as just being sad. Feeling depressed is a normal human emotion but becomes far more severe when a person has thoughts or acts of suicide. This is the main difference between sadness and depression.

'Eww..' is what they yell when confronted with the evidence that **Edward** has **Encorpresis.**

Encorpresis - The repeated involuntary passage of feces in the most inappropriate places for kids beyond toilet training ages (usually after age of 4). This may cause the child to have low self-esteem which can lead to depression.

Foster is a **Frotteurist**, and he enjoys body contact with others.

Frotteurism - Involves touching and rubbing up against a non-consenting person. This behavior is conducted in crowded places whereas an individual can easily rub and touch others and still escape arrest or notice. The behavior is accompanied by fantasies of an actual relationship between the perpetrator and their victims.

Gina likes the ticking sounds from the clocks, that's the only thing that would calm her down for her **Generalized Anxiety Disorder.**

Generalized Anxiety Disorder - An excessive anxiety and worrying over minor, inconsequential things. A patient can not stop worrying about little things and will usually find new things to worry once the old ones are over.

Harry has **Histrionic Personality Disorder** and also is a big time drama queen.

Histrionic Personality Disorder - Patient feels they must be at the center of the attention at all times. Otherwise, he or she would feel extremely insecure. Patient will go to great lengths to gain or regain the attention of others and may resort to dramatic behavior to do so.

Ivan stays up every night to stare at the starry sky, that's the only benefit he gets from **Insomnia.**

Insomnia - The difficulty of initiating or maintaining sleep that lasts for at least 1 month. The result is significant impairment in social, occupational, or other important areas of functioning. Stress, depression, or other mood related disorders may be the cause.

Because of **Jacksonian Seizure, Jessie** often gets tickled from the invisible man.

Jacksonian Seizure - A form of epilepsy. Abnormal electrical activity in localized areas of the brain causing brief alterations in movement and sensation or nerve functions. Patients experience no change in awareness or alertness when having seizures of this type . The seizures are fleeting and short-lived. Other symptoms are abnormal numbness, crawling sensations over skin, or contractions in different parts of the body.

Katie said: I am not a thief, I am just suffering from **Kleptomania.**

Kleptomania - The recurrent failure to resist the impulse to steal anything in reach without regard to personal need or to the stolen item's value. Patients are motivated only by the sheer excitement and tension they derive from stealing paired with the relief of not being caught.

Thanks to **Luke's Learning Disorder**, he is now the oldest 2nd grader in shcool.

Learning Disorder - The substantially lower learning ability in mathematics, reading, and writing skills relative to one's own age group. This is not considered mental retardation.

Maggie has **Munchausen's Syndrome**
She likes to play patient in real life drama.

Munchausen's Syndrome - The habit of feigning illness with different doctors for the sole purpose of gaining attention from others. In this case, patients often put themselves through unnecessary tests and surgeries while claiming to be ill and even go so far as to try and receive treatment whether it's necessary or not.

Nancy's mom doesn't remember when **Nancy** developed **Narcissistic Personality Disorder**, but she does remember Nancy's first word was "me"!

Narcissistic Personality Disorder - Lacking any empathy, patients exhibit an abnormally large need for admiration that usually started in early adulthood. Consumed by an attitude towards their own self importance and preoccupied by fantasies of their success and admiration from others, patient assumes that others hold them in the same regard.

Unlike most kids, **Oscar** saves up his lunch money to buy hand soap.

Unlike most kids, he has **OCD**.

OCD Obsessive-Compulsive Disorder - Time-consuming and useless compulsions or obsessions that are severe and recurring. Obsessed over the fear of a negative result of something, patient compulsively engages in behavior that is believed to prevent the result from happening. Patients, at some point, discover that these obsessions and compulsions are unreasonable and excessive.

Peter's house has lots of fire extinguishers, because of his **Pyromania.**

Pyromania - The propensity to set fires for nothing other than for one's own pleasure leading to a release of tension. Patients suffering from pyromania tend to be fascinated with and attracted to the fire itself and/or to the situational contexts associated with it such as the reaction of others to the fires that they've set. By setting the fire, patient would be able to release the tension and gain pleasure out of it.

Quentin has **Quadraphobia**

Number 4 was never his lucky number.

Quadraphobia - A specific type of phobia whereas the patient suffers from abnormal and extreme fear of quartets or of being drawn and quartered.

Randy is suffering from **Reading Disorder,** thank God there is television.

Reading Disorder - Part of the learning disorders, this relates to the difficulty to understand written words and sentences but without having mental retardation. A patient's reading ability is substantially below average compared to others in the same age group.

Susan has Split Personality (Dissociative Identity Disorder)

And she never goes by the name Susan.

Dissociative Identity Disorder - Behavior that is recurrently controlled by the presence of two or more distinct identities or personality states. Patient exhibits difficulty in recalling important personal information so great that it can't be attributed to ordinary forgetfulness. Females tend to have more identities (up to 15) than males (up to 8).

Tourette's Syndrome really isn't helping **Tina's** cheerleading career.

Tourette's Disorder - Patient suffers from a variety of vocal and/or motor tics which may happen randomly over time. Vocal tics include loud outbursts (including angry swearing) that is unrelated to any conversation and may occur at anytime and anywhere. Motor tics affecting one or a few muscles are simple in nature such as constant and rapid eye blinking. By definition, the disorder is onset before age 18 and as early as 2 years old. Duration of the disorder may be lifelong with weeks or years of periods of remission.

Urian's dream is to be a quality inspector in the factory like his dad. He doesn't know it comes with the side-effect of **Underload Syndrome.**

Underload Syndrome - A sickness caused by boredom. Lack of meaning or excitement in life may cause this. Underload Syndrome usually leads to "depression". People working in extremely dull jobs have an increased probability of developing the syndrome.

Victor does not admit
that he has **Voyeurism**, but he
knows an awful lot about the neighbors.

Voyeurism - Compulsive behavior of secretly watching others with the intent of deriving sexual arousal. Patient will achieve or seek to achieve sexual satisfaction by secretly observing people engaged in sex. This behavior tends to be chronic and onsets typically before age 15.

Warren wants to be a novelist even though he has Written Expression Disorder.

Disorder of Written Expression - Causes writing skills to be substantially much lower than compared to others in patient's own age group. Normally occurring in or around the 2nd grade, this occasionally happens in older children or young adults. Patients demonstrate a combination of difficulties in composing written texts as evidenced by errors in punctuation and grammar, misspelled words, and nearly illegible handwriting. Reading and mathematical disorders commonly accompany it.

Xander said he loves water, but others say he is **Xerophobic.**

Xerophobia - A specific phobia. In this case, the patient suffers from the fear of dryness. Exposing the patient to a dry environment may cause an immediate anxiety response, even though the patient may recognize the fear is unreasonable. Obsessive Compulsive Disorder also commonly occurs in phobia patients.

Youth Violence has become a big problem for **Yoshi**--he has no one left to bully.

Youth Violence - Serious violence that occurs between children or young adults who are ages 10 to 24. This includes behaviors such as bullying, verbal assault, or hitting others. The perpetrators of youth violence may use these abusive behaviors to control those they are targeting.

Because of **Zoophobia**,
Zach does not like animals very much.

Zoophobia - A type of phobia where a great fear of animals is developed. This may cause anxiety, panic attack, or fainting when exposed to animals.

A Note on the Author

Joey sometimes thinks he suffers from Hallucinations. He likes making drawings of his imaginary friends and you just met 26 of them!

Hallucination- A deeply distorted perception of the current reality that is so strong that it is accompanied by a belief that what is perceived is actual reality. Hallucinations are typically sensory experiences causing the sufferer to feel, see, smell, hear, and/or taste that which isn't really there.